The 1960 Motor Show held at London's Earl's Court between 19th and 29th October. In the right foreground is a Rolls-Royce Silver Cloud II convertible by H. J. Mulliner while the Hillman stand features Series III Minx saloons and convertibles and a Husky estate car. Opposite Vauxhall's stand *opposite (on the left) is a white and yellow Velox on the* DB4.

CLASSIC MOTOR CARS

Jonathan Wood

Shire Publications Ltd

CONTENTS

Set in 9 point Times roman and printed in Great Britain by C. I. Thomas & Sons (Haverfordwest) Ltd, Press Buildings, Merlins Bridge, Haverfordwest, Dyfed.

Editorial Consultant: Michael E. Ware, Curator of the National Motor Museum, Beaulieu.

AUTHOR'S NOTE

For the purposes of this book the classic car period is taken as the thirty years from 1945, when the Second World War ended, until 1975, the year in which the British Leyland Motor Corporation was nationalised, since which time the British motor industry has been transformed.

With the exception of the front cover picture, which is reproduced by courtesy of the National Motor Museum, Beaulieu, all the photographs in this book are from the author's collection.

COVER: *The Warwick-built Healey, one of the new makes to emerge in the post-war years. This is a 1947 example, with body by Elliot of Reading, Berkshire. Powered by a 2.4 litre Riley engine, the Healey was the fastest series production saloon of its day with a top speed of 111 mph (178 km/h), though expensive at £1917. This is an ex-works car, the vehicle in which Count 'Johnnie' Lurani was placed thirteenth in the 1948 Mille Miglia race. The model endured in this form until 1950 and paved the way for the Austin Healey 100 of 1952.*

BELOW: *The Wolverhampton-based Turner company began building its sports cars in 1951 and production lasted until 1966. Chassis were tubular and a variety of engines were fitted including Vauxhall, MG, Austin and, the most powerful, Coventry Climax. Glass-fibre bodywork was the norm and this is a 948 cc model, powered by BMC's ubiquitous A Series engine. Most Turners were exported to the USA.*

The Humber Super Snipe, introduced in 1939, was one of the few British cars to be produced during the war years. When civilian production restarted in 1945 only saloons were on offer and output lasted until 1948. This is one of the tourers, with bodywork by Thrupp and Maberly and oversize 9.00-13 tyres, supplied to the War Office and used by Field Marshal Montgomery, seen here in characteristic posture standing in the rear.

PRE-WAR PRELUDE

Although this book is about cars of the era after the Second World War, it is necessary, in order to give the period a sense of perspective and continuity, briefly to look back to the 1920s.

It was during that decade that the British motor industry came of age, with Morris emerging in 1924 as Britain's leading manufacturer and the famous Bullnose model as the top-selling car. Previously Ford had been by far the largest British manufacturer, with the Model T being mass-produced at a Manchester factory from 1914. However, this reliable, value-for-money product was eclipsed by the introduction, in 1921, of a road-fund licence based on the RAC horsepower of its engine. This was calculated on the bore of the power unit, so a T owner would have to pay £22 a year to tax his Ford while the owner of a Morris Cowley paid only a £12 licence fee. Manufacturers therefore stressed the RAC rating of their model's engines when marketing their cars: Austin Twelve, Singer Nine,

Morris Ten and so on.

Morris's great adversary in the 1920s was Herbert Austin, who had been building cars under his own name since 1905. His most successful model of the inter-war years was the Austin Seven, built between 1922 and 1939. Therefore by the end of the 1920s the market was dominated by three makes, Morris, Austin and Singer, though the influence of Singer was to wain during the 1930s.

Although British car production fell in 1931/2 as a result of the world economic depression, it was still sufficient in 1932 to overtake France, until then Europe's premier car maker. In the same year Ford, after a decade of suffering from the horsepower tax, introduced its Eight model, a small purpose-built car for the European market produced at a new factory at Dagenham, Essex. It was to give the American-owned company a renewed grip on the British market, which it still holds today. Morris output dipped in the early 1930s but the firm

3

ABOVE: *A unique car, the 1952 prototype RGS Atalanta, with John Griffith (who was responsible for the Ford V8 JAG special of 1950-2). The RGS's creator was Richard Shattock, who had taken over the spare parts from the pre-war Atalanta sports car, refined the concept and went into limited production between 1952 and 1956. He was also one of the first British car makers to offer glass-fibre bodywork.*

fought back with its own Eight in 1934, effectively a copy of the successful small Ford. By the end of the decade Morris Motors was once again Britain's principal motor manufacturer. The firm had also grown considerably by acquisition, having bought Wolseley in 1926 and Riley in 1938, along with many component suppliers. The popular MG (Morris Garages) sports-car line had also emerged in the 1920s.

Although Austin maintained its second place behind Morris in motor-car manufacturing, it was being challenged at the outbreak of the Second World War in 1939 by Ford, by a revitalised Standard company, by the Hillmans, Humbers and Sunbeams of the Rootes Group, created in the 1930s, and by Vauxhall, taken over by the huge American General Motors Corporation in 1925.

These big six manufacturers dominated the car market though there were other, smaller firms of significance. Rolls-Royce was still building its stately saloons, while the SS company, which had been making cars only since 1931, was producing stylish and distinctive open and closed models. A resurgent Rover company offered well built middle-class saloons and Alvis found there was a consistent demand for its well engineered high-speed tourers. The post-war motor-car business was destined to be very interesting.

BELOW: *The MGA, introduced in 1955, was a great favourite in America and remained in production until 1962. Offered initially in 1489 cc form, capacity was increased to 1588 cc in 1959 and to 1622 cc in 1962. It was first available as a roadster, but in 1956 came this coupé version. The twin cam model of 1958-60 is almost identical, with the exception of handsome centre-lock Dunlop wheels.*

Featured at the 1953 Motor Show, although it never went into production, the Singer SMX was unusual in using glass-fibre bodywork. Aimed at the American market, hence the left-hand drive, it was powered by the make's well established 1½ litre single overhead-camshaft four-cylinder engine. The firm was taken over by Rootes in 1955 and lasted until 1970.

PERFORMANCE MOTORING

British car production virtually ceased during the Second World War but when output restarted in 1945 the motor industry was directed to export its cars. The demands of fighting the Second World War had exhausted Britain's currency reserves and a balance of payments programme was a key policy of Clement Attlee's post-war Labour government. This entailed exports in the first instance to Australia, New Zealand and South Africa but later the vast potential of the American market was realised, with British sports cars making available the delights of open-air motoring.

MG was in the vanguard of this offensive but the only car suitable for production was the delightful but archaic TC, the design of which had its origins in the early 1930s. A few found their way across the Atlantic but the version that sold best was the TC's 1950 derivative, the TD, which had independent front suspension, while in 1954 came the TF, which lasted only until 1955. Fortunately by then MG had received the approval of its BMC parent (the Austin and Morris companies

having merged in 1952 to form the British Motor Corporation) for a long awaited replacement in the shape of the MGA, which was as modern as the T Series cars were archaic.

The A was launched at the Le Mans twenty-four hour race though because the June announcement date had to be put back until the autumn the cars were entered in EX 182 guise. The cars were placed twelfth and seventeenth and one crashed but the MGA was an unqualified success and by the time the model ceased production in 1962 over a hundred thousand examples had been produced, making it the world's best-selling sports car. This included a short-lived twin overhead-camshaft version, which developed a reputation for unreliability.

The MGA was an out-and-out sports car but its replacement, the MGB, was much more of a high-speed tourer, although a very successful one. The bodywork was new while the engine was a 1.8 litre derivative of the A's unit. The MGB was due for replacement in the late 1960s but because of the problems of

Healey was one of the new British makes to appear after the Second World War. Production of Riley-engined models began in 1947 and this is the Silverstone of 1949. Intended to circumvent the introduction of double purchase tax (66⅔ per cent) on automobiles costing more than £1000, the Silverstone cost £975 before tax. Note the horizontally mounted spare wheel, intended to serve also as a rear bumper!

BMC, which was effectively taken over by Leyland Motors to create British Leyland in 1968, the MGB eventually had an eighteen-year production run. By the time that it ceased production in 1980, over half a million examples had been built but following its demise MG's world-famous Abingdon factory closed.

The Austin Healey 100 followed the MG as an export to America. The veteran rally enthusiast and driver Donald Healey began building sports cars at Warwick in 1946. His first models, with Riley engines, were fast, being capable of over 100 miles per hour (160 km/h), but production was low and the cars were expensive. Healey realised that he needed a lighter, cheaper car or he would go out of business. He therefore created the Austin-engined Healey 100, the prototype appearing at the 1952 Motor Show. Leonard Lord, BMC's chairman, saw the blue prototype on display there and proposed that the model be mass-produced by BMC and renamed the *Austin* Healey. Production began the following year and the car's performance, rugged qualities and good looks were much admired in America. In 1956 the 2.4 litre four-cylinder engine was replaced by a 2.6 litre six-cylinder engine, which was enlarged to 3 litres in 1959, when the car was renamed the Austin Healey 3000. By then the Big Healey was a versatile performer in track and rally events but as the decade proceeded the car was becoming increasingly uncompetitive and the new American safety regulations, due for introduction in 1968, led to the ending of production.

Although the Big Healey was no more, the name remained alive a further three years because in 1958 Healey produced the 'Frog Eye' Sprite with a 948 cc Austin engine. The little car proved a great success and, in 1961, there came an MG version named the Midget. With the creation of British Leyland, the new management decided to discontinue the Austin Healey name and the Sprite ceased production in 1970 though the Midget continued until 1979.

BMC was not the only British manufacturer successfully to exploit the American sports-car market. In 1952 the Triumph company revealed the first of an open two-seater line which emerged as the TR2 the following year. Triumph, bankrupted in 1939, was bought by the Standard company in 1945, which is why the TR2 was powered by the 1991 cc engine from the Standard Vanguard saloon. The TR2 was the first of a long and distinguished line. The TR3, of the same capacity but developing more power, arrived in 1956, while the TR4, with new bodywork styled by Michelotti, followed in 1961. Engine capacity was increased to 2138 cc and production lasted until 1965. That year came the TR4A, with independent rear suspension, but this was replaced in 1967 by the TR5, with a 2½ litre six-cylinder engine, though with similar bodywork. This lasted for a little under two years, until the TR6 arrived, with new Karmann-designed bodywork, and this remained in production until 1976, making it one of the biggest-selling of all the TR sports cars. Its 1975 replacement sold in even greater numbers, a total of

ABOVE: *Designed for the American market, the Austin Healey 100 appeared in four-cylinder form in 1953. In 1956 came the 100/6, shown here, with a 2.6 litre six-cylinder engine and costing £1144. Capable of just over 100 mph (160 km/h) this version lasted until 1959, when the engine's capacity was increased to 3 litres and it was renamed the Austin Healey 3000. It continued in this form until the end of 1967.*

BELOW: *Donald Healey followed the success of the Big Healey with the Sprite in 1958. This popular model, with its 'Frog Eye' front, cost £648 and was powered by BMC's A series four-cylinder engine. Note the lack of boot lid; access to the rear compartment was gained by moving the seat backs forward. The glass-fibre hardtop proved a popular option, costing an extra £49.*

ABOVE: *Triumph's sports-car line began with the TR2 in 1953 and this is the TR4 of 1961 with the full-width body by Giovanni Michelotti. However, it was essentially the familiar TR3/3A with a 2138 cc four-cylinder engine. Independent rear suspension followed with the TR4A of 1965, with a six-cylinder engine fitted in 1967 for the redesignated TR5. The TR6 of 1969, by contrast, had a new Karmann-styled body.*

BELOW: *The Elite was Lotus's first proper road car and also had the distinction of being the world's first glass-fibre monocoque. Introduced at the 1957 Motor Show it did not enter production until the end of 1958, with bandleader Chris Barber owning the first car. Styled by Colin Chapman's friend Peter Kirwan-Taylor, the Elite was powered by a 1216 cc Coventry Climax engine. This is the prototype, pictured in the grounds of Alexandra Palace, London, prior to the 1957 Show.*

111,648 examples being built, but from its announcement the TR7 proved visually controversial and there were problems with the 2 litre single overhead-camshaft four-cylinder engine. Originally it was available only in coupé form but in 1980 came an open version. The Rover V8 engined TR8 was manufactured for a brief period but both models ceased production in 1981. These were the last of the British mass-produced sports cars and three years later, in 1984, the Triumph name disappeared from the British motor industry.

The MGs, Triumphs and Austin Healeys were successful but conventional sports cars but Colin Chapman, who began building his Lotus sports cars

ABOVE: *The Swallow Doretti was built at Walsall Airport in 1954 and 1955. Powered by the Triumph TR2 2 litre engine, the model was expensive at £1102, £215 more than the Triumph. Although its top speed was nearly 100 mph (160 km/h), the Doretti was not a success and the parent company, Tube Investments, decided to end production after only two years.*

BELOW: *The Michelotti-styled Triumph Stag, intended to challenge the luxury cars from Europe, appeared in 1970. This GT was powered by a 3 litre V8-engine, the result of a union of two 1½ litre four-cylinder overhead-camshaft units designed by Triumph for Saab. Suspension was all independent. Unfortunately this 120 mph (193 km/h) car developed a reputation for unreliability; only 25,877 were made and an export market failed to materialise. Production ceased in 1977.*

behind his father's North London hotel in 1953, was far from conventional. Initially these sports racers were offered in kit form but in 1957 came the Elite, the world's first glass-fibre monocoque sports car, with a 1.2 litre Coventry Climax engine. The Elite looked sensational but eventually Lotus was losing £100 on every one it built. It was replaced, in 1963, by the open two-seater Elan, with all-independent suspension and a Ford-based 1498 cc, soon enlarged to 1588 cc, twin overhead-camshaft engine. A +2 coupé version appeared in 1967, by which time the firm had moved to Hethel, Norfolk, following a spell at Cheshunt, Hertfordshire. The same year came the mid-engined Europa, with its 1½ litre

9

Renault R16 power unit located in the manner of Colin Chapman's Grand Prix cars. This coupé, which was powered by the Elan's twin overhead-camshaft engine from 1971, was built until 1975.

But by far the most successful British sports cars to appear during the 1950s and 1960s were the Jaguars of William Lyons. The first of the post-war line, the XK 120, was exhibited at the 1948 Motor Show with a new 3.4 litre twin overhead-camshaft six-cylinder engine. The magnificent XK, its name reflecting its top speed of over 120 mph (193 km/h), also had good looks and, being a Jaguar, was competitively priced at £1263. The 120's success took Jaguar by surprise and production at the Coventry factory did not get into its stride until 1950. Four years later, in 1954, the 120 was replaced by the XK 140, with similar bodywork and rack and pinion steering. This was in turn replaced in 1957 by the XK 150, whose name did not, however, reflect its top speed, which was around 135 mph (217 km/h). Styling was similar to its predecessors and braking was improved by the fitting of all-round disc brakes. Although it initially had a 3.4 litre engine, a 3.8 litre version of the XK power unit was introduced in 1960. Output continued until 1961, when the model was replaced by the E-type.

In 1950 a team of XK 120s, with unofficial backing from Jaguar, was entered for the famous Le Mans twenty-four hour race. One car dropped out after twenty-one hours but the remaining two were placed in twelfth and fifteenth positions, and this outcome convinced Lyons that a specially built sports racer could win the event. The result was the C-type, and a team was entered for the 1951 race. Two cars retired but a third, driven by Peter Whitehead and Peter Walker, won the race, the first British victory at Le Mans since 1935. There were four more Jaguar victories, in 1953, 1955, 1956 and 1957, repeating Bentley's successes of the 1920s. The C-type endured until 1953 when it was replaced by the D-type, a handsome two-seater capable of around 170 mph (273 km/h). Although Jaguar officially withdrew from racing in 1956, the following year the winning D-type was entered by the Edinburgh-based Ecurie Ecosse racing team, with privately entered Jaguars in third and fourth places. A road-going version of the D-type, named the XK SS, was offered, briefly, for public sale in 1957.

It was the D-type that provided the starting point for Jaguar's next sports car, introduced in 1961. The E-type, perhaps the greatest of all Jaguar sports cars, was powered by a 3.8 litre version of the long-running XK engine. It looked sensational, unlike any other sports car, had a

The final version of the Jaguar line begun with the XK120 was the XK150, which appeared in 1957 in fixed and drophead coupé forms, the two-seater roadster appearing in 1958. Disc brakes were introduced with the 150 and it was available with the standard 3.4 litre engine, or the more powerful S version. A 3.8 litre engine was available in 1959, capable of over 135 mph (217 km/h) and built until 1961.

ABOVE: *The Jaguar twin overhead-camshaft XK unit, introduced in 1948 and still being manufactured, has been in production longer than any other British engine. First produced in 3.4 litre form, a 2.4 litre version came in 1955, followed by a 3.8 litre in 1959. The larger capacity 4.2 litre engine of 1965 is shown here.*

BELOW: *The 150 mph (241 km/h) E-type Jaguar. Introduced at the 1961 Geneva Motor Show, the model was available in coupé and roadster forms. Suspension was all independent, an unusual feature for a British car of its day. Production lasted until 1975, though from 1971 the six-cylinder engine was replaced by a V12 unit. The bonnet is forward-hinging, permitting excellent access to the engine and front suspension.*

top speed of 150 mph (241 km/h) and sold for £1,550 in coupé form, while the roadster version was slightly cheaper at £1,480. For 1965 a 4.2 litre engine replaced the original unit and, although top speed remained about the same, acceleration was improved. A Series 2 version, with modifications tailored to the all-important American safety regulations, appeared in 1968 and in the Series 3 car of 1971 the six-cylinder engine was replaced by a 5.3 litre V12 unit. The E-type continued to be built in this form until 1975 and with its demise the Jaguar sports car line ended. Its XJS successor was purely a grand tourer.

Jaguar's XK 120 had achieved 132.596 mph (213.4 km/h) on the Jabbeke-Aeltre autoroute in Belgium in 1949 and the Rootes Group also tested its sports model. In 1953 Rootes introduced the Alpine, a two-seater version of the Sunbeam-Talbot 90. It attained over 120 mph (193 km/h) and was named after the Alpine Trials, where the make was so successful. That version lasted until 1955 but four years later, in 1959, came a purpose-built sports car, the two-seater Alpine, powered by a 1600 cc version of the Rootes four-cylinder engine, which was to make an impact on both sides of the Atlantic. It lasted until 1968, by which time it was 1725 cc powered. A

version of the car, specifically geared to the requirements of the American market, was the Sunbeam Tiger, introduced in 1964. Based on the Series IV Alpine bodyshell, it had a 4.2 litre Ford V8 engine. Initially available in left-hand drive form, it was named after the Sunbeam in which Henry Segrave took the world land speed record at 152.33 mph (245 km/h) in 1926. The Tiger subsequently went on sale in Britain but lasted only until 1967. It was in that year that Chrysler took control of the Rootes Group and a sports car with a Ford V8 engine went against the corporate grain.

The Sunbeam Tiger had been inspired by the V8-engined AC Cobra, which was introduced in 1962 and was a derivative of AC's 1954 Ace sports car, available with the firm's long-running 2 litre six-cylinder overhead-camshaft engine or the potent but costly Bristol unit of a similar capacity. But Bristol ceased to produce its engine after 1961 and two years later AC discontinued its own engine. Although a Ford Zephyr engine was available there were few takers and it seemed that the Ace would cease production. But an American racing driver, Carroll Shelby, who had co-driven the winning DBR1 Aston Martin at Le Mans in 1959, suggested fitting a big V8 engine in the Ace. The name Cobra came to him

Sunbeam introduced its two-seater Alpine sports car in 1959 and production lasted until 1968. Powered by the Rootes Group's four-cylinder engine, when important American sales began to flag in the early 1960s Ian Garrad, the company's east coast manager in the USA, developed the idea of a Ford 4.2 litre V8-engined version. The Tiger entered production in 1964 and lasted until 1967, latterly in 4.7 litre form.

ABOVE: *The AC Ace, available with a Bristol engine until 1961, was thereafter offered with a 2.6 litre Ford Zephyr unit in varying degrees of tune. As this was shallower than the Bristol engine, which was unusually deep, a lower bonnet line was possible and the model's looks improved accordingly. Top speed was over 120 mph (193 km/h) and it was this version that paved the way for the V8-engined Cobra.*
BELOW: *Frazer Nash cars were chain-driven before the Second World War though conventional transmission was adopted afterwards. Production began in 1948 and these cars were the work of BMW designer Fritz Fiedler. They had tubular chassis with transverse-leaf independent front suspension and rear torsion bars. The engine was the BMW 328-derived Bristol unit. This is a 1950 Mille Miglia model, of which no two are alike. The hatch on the side of the wing is for the spare wheel. Frazer Nash cars were built until 1956.*

one night in a dream. A prototype was built and it proved a success. Cars, without engines, were shipped from Britain to California, where a Ford 4.2 litre V8 was fitted. Capacity was increased to 4.7 litres and eventually a 7 litre V8 was used. This 160 mph (257 km/h) car ceased production in 1968.

The Bristol engine took its name from the car produced by the Bristol Aeroplane Company which was introduced in 1947. But the design did not originate from the firm's Filton works but from Germany. After the Second World War, details of the Munich-based BMW company's designs were brought to Britain by H. J. Aldington, who had sold the cars in Britain under the name Frazer Nash-BMW before the war. The Bristol 400, the first of the line, was effectively a BMW 326 chassis, 328 engine and 327-derived body. It was joined, in 1948, by

13

ABOVE: *David Brown acquired the Lagonda company and Aston Martin in 1948. The first Aston Martin to reflect this union was the DB2 of 1950 which used the 2.6 litre Lagonda twin overhead-camshaft six-cylinder engine. Lagonda entered production in 1948 and this four-seat drophead coupé was built until 1952. Although Lagondas are no longer made, Aston Martin has preserved it as a model rather than marque name.*

BELOW: *The Aston Martin DB4 with body styled by Touring of Milan and powered by a 3.6 litre twin overhead-camshaft six-cylinder engine. Suspension is by wishbones at the front while a live rear axle with trailing arms is employed as the de Dion unit originally intended could not be used for production. The DB4's price at the time of its 1958 launch was £3976.*

the aerodynamically efficient 401 and subsequent models were refinements on this theme. The BMW engine lasted until 1961, when it was replaced by a Chrysler V8 unit, which is still used.

All past and present Bristols are good examples of what are now called *Gran Turismo* models, better known by the initials GT. These were two-door high-performance cars but with closed rather than open bodywork and with room for children, at least, in the back. The concept originated on the continent of Europe and had been developed there in the 1930s, and it was the Italians who successfully developed the theme in the early post-war years. Apart from Bristol, another early exponent of the GT in Britain was Aston Martin. This old-established company had been bought by David Brown, a Huddersfield-based gear and tractor manufacturer, in 1948. He also acquired Lagonda the same year, attracted by the potential of a Bentley-designed 2.6 litre twin overhead-camshaft six-cylinder engine. This was installed in an existing Aston Martin chassis which was fitted with an attractive two-door closed body and named the DB2 (for David Brown). The model was enlarged and refined in subsequent years and lasted until 1959. It had been replaced the previous year by the DB4, a completely new model with a 3.6 litre twin overhead-

camshaft six-cylinder engine, and was magnificently styled by the Italian Touring company. The performance of this 140 mph (225 km/h) Grand Tourer matched its appearance. It was replaced in 1963 by the 4 litre DB5, while in 1965 came the DB6, with longer wheelbase and spoiler lip at the rear, and this lasted until 1970.

The DB6's engine and gearbox were also used in the DBS, introduced in 1967, though it had been intended to use a new V8 engine then under development. This engine finally appeared in 1970 and was a 5.3 litre unit with twin overhead cam-shafts for each cylinder bank. With a top speed of 145 mph (233 km/h), a derivative of this model is still being manufactured as Britain's fastest production car.

Aston Martin is the only British manufacturer to have won the World Sports Car Championship. This was attained in 1959, the year in which David Brown also achieved his ambition of winning the Le Mans twenty-four hour race. Carroll Shelby and Roy Salvadori drove the DBR1 to victory, and another example was in second place. By 1972 Sir David Brown (as he had become in 1968) found that he could no longer shoulder the burden of a loss-making company and sold the firm, but despite a chequered corporate history Aston Martin is still in business.

The sports racing Aston Martin DBR1. It was with this model, introduced in 1957, that the firm won the Le Mans twenty-four hour race in 1959. The winning car averaged 112.5 mph (181 km/h) and was powered by a 3 litre twin overhead-camshaft six-cylinder engine. Another example was in second place. Aston Martin's main challenge came from Ferrari, with the Italian cars coming in third, fourth, fifth and sixth places.

ABOVE: *The long-established Daimler company produced a great variety of models in the post-war years and this is one of the most memorable. The Barker Special Sports model, with bench-type front seat and transverse rear one, was so called because Daimler had bought the Barker coachbuilding company in 1938. Introduced in 1949, it cost £2560 and remained available until 1953. It was powered by a 2½ litre six-cylinder engine and used a preselector gearbox with fluid flywheel. In 1960 BSA, which had owned Daimler since 1910, sold the firm to Jaguar.*
BELOW: *Owners of classic cars often join the one-make club which caters for the vehicle in which they are interested. There they meet like-minded enthusiasts who can exchange advice about the model's advantages and shortcomings. The availability of spares is another important benefit. Such a club is the Bristol Owners' and this BMW-derived Bristol 400 was photographed at an event held at Blenheim Palace.*

The most popular British post-war car, the Morris Minor. Introduced in 1948, it was designed by Alec Issigonis, who was later responsible for the Mini Minor. Produced in saloon and convertible forms, in 1954 it was joined by the wood-framed Traveller (produced until 1971). The split windscreen, introduced because the means of manufacturing a curved one did not then exist, lasted until 1956.

CLASSIC SALOONS

The 1948 Motor Show, the first to be held for ten years, was significant not only for the first appearance of the XK 120 Jaguar, but also for that of the Morris Minor. It was designed almost single-handedly by Alec Issigonis, and work on the project had begun during the Second World War under the code name Mosquito. Originally a flat four-cylinder engine, of similar layout to the Volkswagen Beetle's, was projected but because of cost considerations the existing 918 cc side-valve unit from the Morris Eight was adopted. The Minor, with its outstanding road holding and distinctive rounded contours, soon attained popularity all over the world. Following Morris's 1952 merger with Austin, the A30's 803 cc overhead-valve engine replaced the Eight unit, while for 1957 capacity was increased to 948 cc and the model renamed the Minor 1000. There was another capacity increase, to 1098 cc, in 1963 and

the model remained in production until 1971. The millionth Minor appeared in January 1961; it was the first British car to reach this figure.

Alec Issigonis also designed the Mini Minor, sold under the Austin and Morris names at its appearance in 1959. Its transverse engine, front-wheel drive and 10 inch (254 mm) wheels have since changed the course of small car design throughout the world. It is still in production today, a classic design if ever there was one. The faster Cooper version of the Mini was introduced in 1961 though the model was discontinued in 1971 following the creation of British Leyland. Competition successes for the works Mini Cooper S included triumphs in the Monte Carlo rallies of 1964, 1965 and 1967, outstanding wins for the little cars. Ford's Cortina Lotus and GT models also achieved success in competition in the 1960s. Both derived from the popular Cortina family

saloon, introduced in 1962, with the faster versions appearing the following year. The 105 mph (169 km/h) Cortina Lotus was powered by the Ford-based twin overhead-camshaft 1588 cc engine as used in the Lotus Elan. Finished in white with distinctive green body stripes and using light aluminium body panels, the Lotus soon acquired an enviable reputation on road and track. Equally successful, though slower, was the Cortina GT, powered by a mildly tuned version of the 1500 cc pushrod engine option. A Cortina GT won the 1964 East African Rally while the following year a Cortina Lotus won the European Touring Car Championship and the 1966 RAC Rally.

Another saloon car with a powerful performance was the medium-sized 2.4 litre Jaguar, introduced in 1955 and destined for a fourteen-year production life. It proved to be the best-selling Jaguar of the post-war years until the XJ6 appeared in 1968. In 1959 a Mark II version with thinner window pillars and a new radiator grille was introduced. In addition to the existing 2.4 and 3.4 litre XK engines there was a new 3.8 litre power unit. The model endured until 1969. Jaguar was first and foremost a manufacturer of closed models, with the stylish sports cars being of only secondary importance, and the famous 3.4 litre XK twin overhead-camshaft engine was conceived so that the big, roomy 1950 Mark VII saloon would be a 100 mph (160 km/h) car, with the use of the engine in the XK 120 as a sideline. The saloon was replaced by the similar Mark VIII in 1957 and the distinctive profile was discontinued when the 3.8 litre Mark IX ceased production in 1961. The bulbous Mark X that replaced it, with all-independent suspension, was not one of Jaguar's more stylish cars.

Slower than the Jaguars were the well finished and comfortable Rover 'Auntie' saloons. The 75, introduced in 1950, had a 2.1 litre six-cylinder engine with unusual overhead inlet and side exhaust layout. The 2 litre four-cylinder 60 followed in 1954, the same year that the 75 was replaced by the 2.3 litre 90. In 1957 came the 105S, a more powerful version of the 90, and the 105R (for Roverdrive), which employed a curious semi auto-

ABOVE: *The Cortina Lotus (not the Lotus Cortina) was available only in two-door right-hand-drive form, with its distinctive white bodywork with green side stripe and Lotus badges on the rear wings and radiator grille. A 1588 cc twin overhead-camshaft engine gave a top speed of around 100 mph (160 km/h). At the model's launch in 1963 it cost £1100 and output lasted until the Mark I Cortina ceased production in 1966.*
BELOW: *Ford introduced its 1½ litre Consul in 1950. This four-door saloon was also offered in two-door drophead coupé form from 1953, with a power-operated hood as an optional extra. The conversion was made for Ford by Carbodies of Coventry. This Mark I car lasted until 1956, when it was replaced by a Mark II version which was also available as a convertible.*

ABOVE: *Jaguar's mainstay of the classic period was the 2.4 litre saloon, introduced in 1955, a 3.4 litre model appearing in 1957. The more attractive 1960 Mark II, with slimmer door pillars and a new radiator grille also had a new 3.8 litre engine.*

BELOW: *Alvis had been building cars since 1919 but after the Second World War concentrated on aero engine and military vehicle production. However car production, albeit much reduced, did continue; this is the TD21 of 1959 with coachwork by Park Ward. A 3 litre six-cylinder engine was used and derivatives of this model remained in production until 1967 when production of all Alvis cars at the firm's Coventry works ceased.*

ABOVE: *The final version of the Rover P4 range was the 110, introduced in 1963 but built only until 1964. Until the 110 the series had aluminium doors, bonnet and boot lid but almost all the 110s, with the exception of the first few, had all-steel bodywork. Its engine is a 123 brake horsepower 2.6 litre six-cylinder unit with twin SU carburettors. Overdrive was a standard fitment.*

BELOW: *Big Humbers of the late 1940s were the Super Snipe and the long-wheelbase Imperial. This is a Mark III version of the latter, a body style which was introduced in 1948 and lasted until 1952. Under the long bonnet is a 4 litre six-cylinder side-valve engine. This six-seater Mark III of 1950 had a column gear change, with bench-type front seat.*

The Rover 75 was the inspiration for the Marauder, made in Birmingham between 1950 and 1952. Produced by Wilks, Mackie and Company, fifteen examples were built. Pictured with the prototype Marauder are George Mackie, who became head of Land-Rover Special Products Division; Peter Wilks, subsequently Rover's technical director; and Richard Mead, who bodied the first four cars. Subsequent examples had bodies by Abbey Panels of Coventry. A 2.1 litre six-cylinder engine was used.

matic gearchange. In 1960 the previous models were discontinued and replaced by the 2.6 litre 100 and the 80, which had a 2.3 litre Land-Rover four-cylinder engine. These were replaced in 1963 by the 90 and the 110, also of 2.6 litres, but these ceased production in 1964, when the long-running P4 series was discontinued after fourteen years and the much lauded 2000 was introduced, aimed at a younger clientele. It was distinctively styled and mechanically sophisticated with a 2 litre (2.2 from 1973) four-cylinder overhead-camshaft engine and de Dion rear axle with inboard disc brakes.

In some respects the P4 Rover could be regarded as a 'poor man's Bentley' for the discreetly luxurious interior of the Mark VI Bentley had its counterpart in the more prolific and cheaper saloons from Solihull. Rolls-Royce, which had owned Bentley since 1931, had decided that, rather than producing its cars in chassis form only as it had done in pre-war days, it would offer them with standardised steel bodywork. It was to be first applied to the Bentley Mark VI of 1946, which was powered by a 4.2 litre

six-cylinder engine which, like the Rover, had an overhead inlet and side exhaust unit. This shape lasted until 1955, after 1953 being designated the R type, and there was a Rolls-Royce Silver Dawn equivalent. In 1955 came the Rolls-Royce Silver Cloud, along with a Bentley S Series car, and this 4.9 litre model was six-cylinder powered until the introduction of a 6.2 litre V8 engine in 1959, though there was no external evidence of the new power source. In 1966 came a replacement, the Silver Shadow, destined to be the best-selling Rolls-Royce since the Silver Ghost of 1907-25. When the company was bankrupted by the 1971 RB 211 aero-engine debacle, the viability of the Shadow, the first unitary construction Rolls-Royce, and the first with all-independent suspension and disc brakes, tided the firm over the most crucial phase in its history.

Nearly all the British cars to appear in the immediate post-war period were developed from previous models. One exception, however, was Jowett's Javelin saloon, introduced in 1947. Designed during the war by Gerald Palmer, the new model had all-round torsion-bar

ABOVE: *One of the special racing Jupiters produced by the Jowett company of Bradford. Unlike the fastback Javelin saloon, in the background, this two-seater has a tubular chassis, designed by Eberan von Eberhorst, who was responsible for the D-type Auto Union Grand Prix car of pre-war days. Also note (extreme right) the CD van, intended for production in 1954 but never built.*

BELOW: *Rolls-Royce introduced the Silver Cloud in 1955 with standardised bodywork by Pressed Steel. It was powered by a 4.9 litre six-cylinder engine, replaced in 1959 by a 6.2 litre V8 (though the car remained identical externally). The Silver Cloud III of 1963, however, had distinctive horizontally mounted twin headlights. This was the last Rolls-Royce, with the exception of the low production Phantom, to have a separate chassis.*

23

ABOVE: *Riley's attractive 1½ litre RM model, introduced in 1945, remained in production for ten years. It had a dark blue radiator badge while the 2½ litre variant had a light blue one. Originally running boards were fitted though these were dispensed with for the 1954 season, when the rear spats and knife-edge wing styling were introduced. The distinctive fabric roof can present problems for modern owners.*

BELOW: *The Coventry-based Lea-Francis company began building cars in 1904. After a chequered financial history the company ceased production in 1953, though it has since been revived. From 1938 engines were similar to the classic Riley pushrod unit and this is a 14 horsepower 1.7 litre four-cylinder model, introduced in 1950. This is the Series VI version, marketed in 1953.*

Triumph's Herald, named after the managing director's boat, was introduced in 1959. It had a backbone chassis as its body was made in sections, after Fisher and Ludlow, who had made Standard Triumph's monocoque hulls, was taken over by the rival BMC. The distinctive styling is by Giovanni Michelotti. This is the 1200 version, introduced in 1961. The Herald was last produced in 1971.

suspension and a 1½ litre flat four-cylinder engine, mounted well forward. The Javelin was a roomy saloon, capable of over 80 mph (129 km/h) and with good fuel economy. Unfortunately the under-capitalised Jowett company made the disastrous decision to produce its own gearboxes rather than let the expert Meadows company make them as they had done hitherto. Consequently there were gearbox problems from 1951 and the unconventional engine also gave some trouble. As Javelin sales began to slump in 1952, Briggs, the firm's body supplier, was asked by Jowett to cease production and the following year the body company was taken over by Ford. A financial reconstruction of the Jowett company followed but it was unable to give Briggs sufficient financial assurances

Austin's A30 dates from 1951 in 803 cc form and was revamped in 1956 as the A35 with 948 cc power unit. This A35 is pictured at the Montlhery autodrome, near Paris, during a successful seven day and night run which began on 1st July 1957. It broke international records by lapping at an average of 74.89 mph (120.5 km/h) for 20,000 kilometres. At the wheel is Gyde Horrocks, secretary of the Cambridge University Automobile Club.

25

The Austin Motor Company's first sortie into the sporting market was with the A40 Sports in 1950, with bodywork by Jensen Motors. But the model was not a great success and only lasted until 1951. This was despite a much publicised round-the-world drive in June of that year; the twenty-one day trip being undertaken by the team seen here, Ralph Sleigh, George Coates, Ronald Jeavons and Alan Hess.

and production never restarted. After forty-three years as a car maker Jowett was no more. The firm also built the Javelin-based sports car named the Jupiter, between 1950 and 1953, which won the 1½ litre class in the twenty-four hour race at Le Mans in 1950, 1951 and 1952.

Contemporary with the Jowett Javelin, and having a similar type of front suspension, was the RM Riley, introduced in 1945. The Coventry-based Riley company had been purchased by Lord Nuffield in 1938 but the new model that appeared immediately after the war bore no outward resemblance to its 1930s counterparts. The lines were inspired by a pre-war German BMW saloon while the front suspension followed Citroën *Traction Avant* practice. The stylish design was complemented by the fitting of a distinctive fabric roof. The 1½ litre Riley engine, whose origins reached back to 1926, was used, while a 2½ litre version of the model appeared in 1946. However, the larger-capacity car remained in production only until 1953, when it was replaced by the Pathfinder, a 100 mph

(160 km/h) saloon, with distinctive right-hand gearchange, but this lasted only until 1957. The 1½ litre survived rather longer until it ceased production in 1955. The Riley name was, from then on, applied to a variety of BMC models. The years of 'badge engineering' had arrived but with the creation of British Leyland in 1968 Riley output had dwindled to a mere 8346 cars a year and the make was discontinued the following year.

Although Triumph cars are no longer built, the make enjoyed enormous success in 1959 with the arrival of the 948 cc Herald. It was unusual because it used a backbone chassis, as its body was built in sections, and the Italian styling by Giovanni Michelotti was much admired. It also had all-independent suspension, a revolutionary feature for a cheap British car, and a remarkably small turning circle. In addition, the bonnet and front wing section was forward opening, which made the engine and front suspension easily accessible. The Herald evolved over the years, with a 1200 cc version appearing in 1961, and this was further

26

ABOVE: *Today the 'two box' hatchback is very familiar, but in 1958, when Austin's A40 appeared, 'three boxes' were the norm. This was the first new model to emerge from the British Motor Corporation and the styling was by the Italian Pinin Farina company. Although there appeared to be no boot there was luggage space behind the rear seat. The 1960 Countryman version had an opening hatchback and the model was produced until 1967. Before then the styling had been transferred to the best-selling front-wheel drive Morris/Austin 1100.*

BELOW: *Hillman had been building the Minx since 1932 and this is the Mark VIII, introduced late in 1954 and produced until 1956. It had a new 1390 cc overhead-valve engine; hitherto all Minxes had used side-valve units. This is the drophead coupé version, a style that continued with the Series I Minx which succeeded it. The Minx lasted until 1970 and the Hillman name disappeared eight years later.*

27

ABOVE: *Vauxhall, owned by the American General Motors Corporation since 1925, introduced its F type Victor, which echoed the American era of chrome and fins of the 1950s, in 1957. It was followed in 1958 by the PA Cresta, with a 2.3 litre six-cylinder engine, (the Victor used a 1½ litre four). This is Vauxhall's Luton factory in 1958, with a procession of Victors followed by a single Cresta.*

BELOW: *Standard introduced the Vanguard in 1948 and the first, fastback, version lasted until 1952. It was replaced by the Vanguard II, a hatchback. An estate car version was introduced almost from the Vanguard I's introduction, though this is a 1954 Vanguard II version of the type used in large numbers by the Royal Air Force. The model lasted until 1955 when replaced by the Vanguard III.*

Armstrong Siddeley had manufactured cars since 1919 though its mainstay was aero engine manufacture. After the Second World War came the Sapphire, introduced in 1953 with a new 3½ litre six-cylinder engine and pre-selector gearbox, though a manual unit was also available. This model, which was the make's best-selling post-war car (over 7500 were built), lasted until 1959. The following year Armstrong Siddeley car production ended following the firm's merger with Bristol to form Bristol Siddeley aero engines.

increased to 1296 cc in 1967. Production ceased in 1971 but there were three derivatives based on the model: the six-cylinder Vitesse and the sporting Spitfire in 1962 and the fastback GT6 in 1966.

Italian styling also benefited the Austin A40 of 1958. When the British Motor Corporation was established in 1952 there were a number of projects in progress at Austin, at Morris/MG/Wolseley and at Riley that were too advanced to be curtailed. Consequently these had to be brought to fruition and the first truly corporate model did not appear until 1958. BMC's head, Leonard Lord, had recognised that in the past many British cars had suffered from poorly executed and unimaginative styling, most of which was loosely based on American designs. He therefore approached the Turin-based Pinin Farina company and the result was the 948 cc

A40 styled like a modern hatchback. The Countryman version even had an opening tailgate. The A40, latterly of 1098 cc, ceased production in 1967 though the handsome Italian lines had by then been applied to BMC's front-wheel drive 1100 model in 1962. For almost a decade, until it ceased production in 1974, the 1100 was Britain's best-selling car. Pinin Farina also designed a larger and more conventional four-door saloon intended to take all the corporate marque names but it lacked the flair of the stylish A40.

Austin still survives as a make but Armstrong Siddeley ceased production in 1960. The firm had produced aero engines since the First World War and after the Second World War its cars — Lancaster, Hurricane, Typhoon and Whitely — were named after aircraft produced by the Hawker Siddeley group. The firm's best-selling car of the 1950s was the

Sapphire, built between 1953 and 1959. Well appointed and comfortable, mostly fitted with a preselector gearbox and later automatic transmission, the Sapphire came between the Mark VI Bentley and the Rover P4 series for comfort. Unfortu-nately it did not sell in sufficient numbers and when Armstrong Siddeley Motors merged with Bristol Aero Engines to form Bristol Siddeley in 1959 it was decided to discontinue automobile manu-facture.

CLUBS AND EVENTS

This book has described some of the cars that have attained collectable status in recent years and the ranks of classic car enthusiasts are growing all the time. Anyone who is interested should go to a Classic Car Show or to one of the many concours gatherings and club meetings that take place all over Britain. Details of these events can be found in the growing number of classic car magazines available from newsagents.

There is no overall club for post-war cars in Britain but there is an excellent selection of one-make clubs and registers which cater for specific makes or models. For those who want to make contact with a car club, *Practical Classics* magazine publishes in its pages a quarterly Register of Motor Vehicle Clubs.

The Ford Popular exemplified the spirit of the famous Model T Ford of 1908 with its four-cylinder side-valve engine, transverse leaf suspension and mechanical brakes. The 'sit-up-and-beg' style of the 1930s appeared on the 10 horsepower Prefect and 8 horsepower Anglia which were produced in the post-war years. In 1953 the Prefect's 1172 cc engine was fitted in the two-door Anglia body shell and the result was this 1953 Popular, which cost just £390 on its introduction.

Hopes for post-war car production lay in Sir Roy Fedden's idea for a new car developed at Cheltenham, Gloucestershire, from 1943 onwards. The Fedden was powered by a rear-mounted air-cooled 1600 cc three-cylinder sleeve-valve engine driving the wheels via a torque converter. But the project ended in 1946 when this, the only prototype, coded 1 Ex, crashed at the nearby Stoke Orchard aerodrome.

FURTHER READING

It is only in relatively recent years that classic cars have received the attention of publishers but today books on them dominate the motoring market. Many relate to specific makes or models but the following are recommended for their approach to the subject in general terms. Most are available new but, if not, they may be borrowed from a public library or can be purchased second-hand. Those who wish to research into any aspect of the classic motor car may use the library of the National Motor Museum at Beaulieu free of charge. This facility is open seven days a week but a prior appointment would be helpful.

Culshaw, David J. *The Motor Guide to Makes and Models*. Temple Press, 1959.
Georgano, G. N. (editor). *The Complete Encyclopedia of Motor Cars*. Ebury Press, 1982.
Nye, Doug. *British Cars of the Sixties*. Thomas Nelson, 1970.
Robson, Graham. *The Post War Touring Car*. Haynes, 1977.
Sedgwick, Michael. *Cars of the Thirties and Forties*. Hamlyn, 1979.
Sedgwick, Michael. *Cars of the Fifties and Sixties*. Newnes, 1983.
Sedgwick, Michael. *The Motor Car 1946-56*. Batsford, 1979.
Wood, Jonathan. *The Enthusiast's Guide to British Post War Classic Cars*. Osprey, 1982.

MAGAZINES

Until 1973 there was no magazine that specifically catered for post-war cars. Then came *Classic Cars*, which today is Britain's best-selling old car magazine. The following publications all deal with cars of the classic era.

Classic Cars, Reed Business Publishing Ltd, Prospect House, 9-13 Ewell Road, Cheam, Surrey SM1 4QQ.
Popular Classics, EMAP, Bushfield House, Orton Centre, Peterborough PE2 0UW.
Practical Classics, PPG Publishing Ltd, 77 High Street, Beckenham, Kent BR3 1AN.
Supercar Classics, FF Publishing, 97 Earls Court Road, London W8 6QH.
Your Classic, Haymarket Publishing Ltd, 38-42 Hampton Road, Teddington, Middlesex TW11 0JE.

PLACES TO VISIT

There are many motor museums in Britain but the following have a classic car content. Intending visitors are advised to find out the times of opening before making a special journey.

British Motor Industry Heritage Trust, Syon Park, Brentford, Middlesex TW8 3JF. Telephone: 081-560 1378.
Caister Castle Motor Museum, Caister-on-Sea, Great Yarmouth, Norfolk. Telephone: Wymondham, Leicestershire (057 284) 251.
Cotswolds Motor Museum, The Old Mill, Bourton-on-the-Water, Cheltenham, Gloucestershire. Telephone: Bourton-on-the-Water (0451) 21255.
Doune Motor Museum, Carse of Cambus, Doune, Perthshire FK16 6HA. Telephone: Doune (0786) 841203.
Lakeland Motor Museum, Holker Hall, Cark in Cartmel, Grange-over-Sands, Cumbria LA11 7PL. Telephone: Flookburgh (044 853) 509.
Manx Motor Museum, Crosby, Isle of Man. Telephone: Marown (0624) 851236.
Midland Motor Museum, Stanmore Hall, Stourbridge Road, Bridgnorth, Shropshire WV15 6DT. Telephone: Bridgnorth (074 62) 61761.
Museum of British Road Transport, St Agnes Lane, Hales Street, Coventry CV1 1NN. Telephone: Coventry (0203) 832425.
Museum of Transport, Kelvin Hall, 1 Bunhouse Road, Glasgow G3 8DP. Telephone: 041-357 3929.
National Motor Museum, John Montagu Building, Beaulieu, Brockenhurst, Hampshire SO4 7ZN. Telephone: Beaulieu (0590) 612345.
Science Museum, Exhibition Road, London SW7 2DD. Telephone: 071 938 8000.
Sparkford Motor Museum, Sparkford, Yeovil, Somerset BA22 7JJ. Telephone: North Cadbury (0963) 40804.
Stratford-upon-Avon Motor Museum, 1 Shakespeare Street, Stratford-upon-Avon, Warwickshire CV37 6RN. Telephone: Stratford-upon-Avon (0789) 69413.
Totnes Motor Museum, Totnes, Devon. Telephone: Dittisham (080 422) 357.